August 2009

Take recip

notes, anecdotes,

images and information.

Add poetry, sketches,

prints and photographs.

Harness youthful talent,

gifted artists and enthusiasm.

Stir well

and

serve fresh

to feed the body and mind.

With best wishes

Dawn &

Philippa

With love

From Dan The Photo men xx

Published by Bosorne Publications

Compilation copyright © Bosorne Publications 2005

This book has been greatly enhanced by wonderful contributions from Ken Symonds, Neil Pinkett, Bren Unwin, Carrie Taylor, Caroline Binch, Don Kirk, Tom Henderson Smith, John Gordon, Stella Billingham-Henderson and Daisy Gibbs. We are truly grateful to them for their kind and generous support.

We would especially like to thank the Cook Book Crew, in particular Jenny Stephens for her cakes, Ben Rowell for the walks, Jo Vickery for the vinaigrette, Stella and Daisy for working indefatigably on the illustrations and design of the book, and all the others for their encouragement. We have been hugely helped by the enthusiasm of Paula Johnson of Headland Printers, and by many of our customers and friends with whom we have shared the idea of this book, and who seem to think that it has merit.

The proof of the pudding……………..!

10% of the profits of this book will help a disabled child in St Just.
Any surplus will be applied to enabling future members of the Cook Book Crew to develop their talents through working on other publications.

Bosorne Publications

The Count House, Bosorne, St Just, Cornwall TR19 7NR
01736 787778

ISBN 0-9550087-0-0

Printed by Headland Printers
Bread Street, Penzance, Cornwall

About The Cook Book

Good smells....of fresh ground coffee....soup cooking....flowers....cakes baking

Since we opened in 2003 The Cook Book has become more a way of life than a business. We are collecting an ever growing adopted family and an increasing number of friends. We treat visitors to our café exactly the same as people who come to our home. Bright, cheerful young staff engage in every aspect of the café-bookshop. Most are excellent cooks. All take great pride in their work.

Fascinating discussions take place at the bar. This is a good place to come alone or with friends. You will be warmly welcomed; there are papers to read and people to talk to. There is a standing exhibition of paintings by Ken Symonds for sale. The dining room is simply furnished, with 5 round tables seating up to 22 people. As far as possible we buy local produce and support local businesses.

"Feeding the body and mind" reflects the combination of bookshop and café. We always have "Poetry at the Cook Book" in our menus. The choice of poems reflects seasons, world events, special days and the area in which we live.

We are open every day except Monday, between 10.00 a.m. and 5.00 p.m. The Cook Book is closed between midday on Christmas Eve and the first Tuesday in February, to refurbish the building and ourselves. We did try serving evening meals but gave up. We are too old.

How it started

The death of Philippa's mother and the sale of her house provided the capital.

Impetus came when David stopped working – and had no pension!

"Let's run a book-café," said Philippa, knowing how well they worked together when first married, running a 60ft sail training vessel in fair weather and foul.

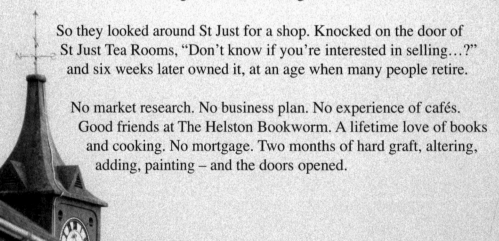

So they looked around St Just for a shop. Knocked on the door of
St Just Tea Rooms, "Don't know if you're interested in selling…?"
and six weeks later owned it, at an age when many people retire.

No market research. No business plan. No experience of cafés.
Good friends at The Helston Bookworm. A lifetime love of books
and cooking. No mortgage. Two months of hard graft, altering,
adding, painting – and the doors opened.

Memorable Events

Knocking down the wall into the servery. Changing from green to white paint

Designing the bar. Jamie building it, surrounded by 4,500 books in boxes

The arrival of the gleaming, steaming coffee machine. Learning to use it

Malcolm filling St Just with sawdust when building bookcases

Hanging Ken Symond's paintings

Joining "Just Arts"

Opening on 5th April 2003. *"We're new here, please be kind"* on the blackboards.
People were, and still are

Opening Bosorne Books on 23rd April. Happy Birthday Mr Shakespeare

St Just Yoga Class's Wednesday teas, coffees and hot chocolates.
Cape Cornwall School Science Department's Friday lunches

Children's birthday parties. Getting re-named
"The love you, love you café" by one family

meeting people
making friends
looking after them

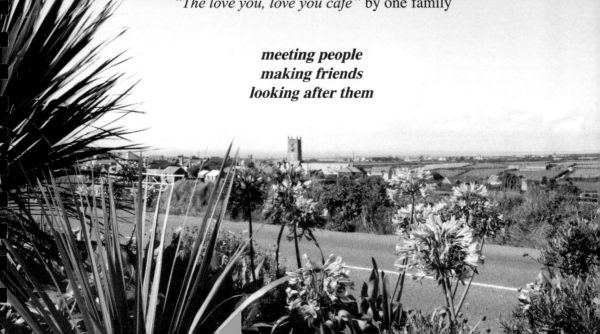

Beyond

Beyond the cliffs of Treen
a secret garden lies – walled, unseen.
There, at the threshold hour of inbetween,
on a throne of sunwarmed stone,
mambled with moss and eglantine,
sits a mage of madritic mien
in vervant robe enrapt, gold broidered, green,
whose musings ever mould and tune
the chantments of that far demesne,
where badgers roll the mellow moonbeam,
and on a drift of gentled dream
a rosesoft peace is elfin strown.

John Gordon
St Just and Penzance

Some people sniff solvents and glue
At the Cook Book we're big sniffers too
   The aroma of beans
     In the coffee machines
Is the flavour for me and for you

Coffee

We serve organic Arabica coffee from Papua New Guinea. It is delicious, and is supplied by Origin, a Cornish family business run by dedicated enthusiasts. Decaffeinated coffee is available.

For the full flavour, first clean your palate with a glass of ice-cold water

Espresso
: a short, black, strong cup that *'stiffens the sinews, summons up the blood'*

Espresso Macchiato
: espresso topped with a dollop of foamed milk

Double Espresso
: two shots of espresso. Not for the faint hearted

Americano
: espresso and hot water. Hot or cold milk to taste. Also known as a normal, regular or flat coffee

Latte
: espresso with hot steamed milk

Cappuccino
: espresso topped with equal amounts of steamed and foamed milk, sprinkled with chocolate powder

Mocha
: espresso mixed with chocolate and steamed milk, topped with foamed milk and sprinkled with chocolate powder

Frappe
: espresso whizzled with ice, cold milk, and white chocolate and vanilla frappe mix

Hot Chocolate
: *'Food of the gods'* chocolate, steamed milk, topped with foamed milk and sprinkled with chocolate powder

organic coffee
227g ℮

ORiGiN™

mill house, trewardreva mill, constantine, falmouth, cornwall, tr11 5qd
ph 01326 340 320   fx 01326 340 660

Best Before End: **20/10/2005**

for storage instructions see rear

"Turkish coffee – black as the devil, hot as hell, pure as an angel and sweet as love"

Cook Book Coffee

A Scottish connoisseur, who has been a regular visitor to Cornwall for many years, has described our coffee as *"The best in Cornwall"*. This boundary has now been extended and we are reputed to *"serve the best cappuccino West of Bristol"*. An exuberant Australian told us it is *"the best ever!"*

Part of the pleasure is visual, for our coffees are served in unique cups and mugs made by local potter, Helen Jay. She lives in Cot Valley, where she has her studio.

Helen's pottery is on sale here.

Real espresso is used in our coffee and walnut cakes. Here is the recipe. You can buy bags of Origin ground Arabica coffee from us.

Coffee and Walnut Cake

175g (6oz) margarine
175g (6oz) caster sugar
175g (6oz) self-raising flour
3 eggs
½ tsp baking powder
85g (3oz) chopped walnuts
½ small cup of strong black coffee (espresso)

Icing
55g (2oz) margarine
3 tbsp milk
225g (8oz) icing sugar sieved
½ small cup of strong black coffee (espresso)

Pre-heat the oven to 160C (325F, gas mark 3)
Place all the cake ingredients into a bowl and beat with a wooden spoon until well mixed (1½-2 minutes)
Place mixture into two greased and lined 18cm (7 inch) cake tins
Bake for 30-40 minutes

To make the icing, place all ingredients into a bowl over a saucepan of hot water
Stir until mixture is glossy
Remove from heat and leave until cool
Beat well until thick
Sandwich cakes together with half the icing and spread the remainder on top
Decorate with walnut halves

Cake Cornwall

Neil Pinkett

Cakes baked here by Jenny Stephens include our favourite, dried apricot and almond; fantastic chocolate fudge, lemon drizzle that melts in your mouth, and coffee and walnut that vanishes as soon as it's been made.

Apricot and Almond Cake

2 tbsp Demerara sugar
30g (1oz) flaked almonds
200g (7oz) dried apricots
250g (8oz) butter
250g (8oz) caster sugar
4 eggs
200g (7oz) self-raising flour
30g (1oz) ground almonds
½ tsp almond essence

Pre-heat the oven to 180C (350F, gas mark 4).
Oil a 20.5cm (8 inch) square tin and
line with non-stick baking paper
Sprinkle sugar and flaked almonds over the paper, then arrange 5oz of dried, finely chopped apricots on the bottom of the tin
Cream the butter and sugar together in a large bowl until light and fluffy
Gradually beat the eggs into the butter mixture, adding a spoonful of flour after each egg
Stir in the remaining flour and flaked almonds
Add the almond essence and the rest of the apricots
Spoon the mixture into the tin. Bake for 1 hour, or until golden and firm
Allow to cool for 15-20 minutes
Turn and remove paper, sprinkle with Demerara sugar and serve

Pumpkin Cake

450g (1lb) grated pumpkin flesh
240ml (8fl oz) sunflower oil
350g (12oz) soft dark brown sugar
3 eggs
125g (5oz) self-raising flour
5ml (1tsp) baking powder
5ml (1tsp) ground cinnamon
5ml (1tsp) ground nutmeg
150g (6oz) chopped walnuts
75g (3oz) sultanas

Whisk eggs and sugar together until light and fluffy, then whisk in the grated pumpkin and the oil
Sift the self-raising flour with the spices and baking powder. Add to the pumpkin mixture, together with the walnuts and sultanas. Mix well
Grease a 900g (2lb) loaf tin and spoon in the mixture
Bake for approximately an hour and a half in a moderate oven – 180C (350F or gas mark 4)
The cake is cooked when a skewer pushed into the centre of the cake comes out clean. Turn out and allow to cool

Serve sliced with butter or clotted cream

Chocolate Fudge Cake

100g (4oz) of butter
175g (6oz) plain dark chocolate, roughly chopped
200g (8oz) caster sugar
2 tsp vanilla essence
2 eggs lightly beaten
125g (5oz) of plain flour sifted

Icing
175g (6oz) icing sugar
2 tbsp cocoa powder
15g (½oz) butter

Pre-heat the oven to 180C (350F, gas mark 4)
Lightly oil and line a 20.5cm (8 inch) square cake tin with grease proof or baking paper
Slowly melt the butter and chocolate together in a large bowl set over a saucepan of simmering water
Stir in the sugar and the vanilla essence, and then the eggs
Fold in the flour
Pour into the tin
Bake for 30 minutes until just set
Remove the cooked mixture from the oven and leave in a tin to cool before turning it out on to a wire rack

Sift the icing sugar and cocoa powder into a small bowl
Make a well in the centre
Place the butter in the well, then gradually add about 2 tbsp of hot water
Mix till smooth
Spread the icing on the cooled cake

Carrot Cake

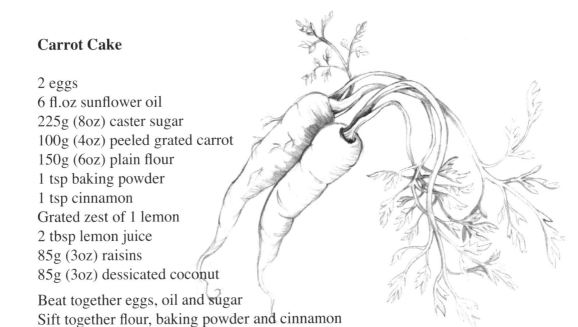

2 eggs
6 fl.oz sunflower oil
225g (8oz) caster sugar
100g (4oz) peeled grated carrot
150g (6oz) plain flour
1 tsp baking powder
1 tsp cinnamon
Grated zest of 1 lemon
2 tbsp lemon juice
85g (3oz) raisins
85g (3oz) dessicated coconut

Beat together eggs, oil and sugar
Sift together flour, baking powder and cinnamon
Mix all the ingredients together and beat until well combined
Put into a greased, floured tin and bake at 190C for about 20 minutes

Lafrowda Pudding

Half a large loaf of yesterday's malt crunch bread, soaked overnight in ½ pint of
mixed milk and water
350g (12oz) mixed fruit
50g (2oz) mixed, chopped candied peel
1 apple, peeled and grated
3 tbsp soft brown sugar
3 tbsp self-raising flour
2 tbsp marmalade
2 eggs
Juice of 1 lemon
1 tsp of cinnamon
½ tsp of nutmeg
120g (4oz) butter

Thoroughly mix all the ingredients except butter. Melt butter and stir ½ into the
mixture. Pour mixture into a greased roasting tin and top with the remaining
butter. Bake at 150C for 1 hour 15 minutes and a final 15 minutes at 180C.
Delicious with large amounts of clotted cream

Lafrowda Day

Lafrowda – Old Cornish name meaning 'The church of the good cross'

St Just used to have a carnival, with decorated bicycles, carnival queens and fabulous floats on tractors, trailers and lorries. Sadly, health & safety regulations and growing insurance costs forced small towns and villages to give up.

Lafrowda Day was born in 1996, the brainchild of Mary-Ann Bloomfield and Bridget Gibbs. They had been asked to include more young people in St Just Music Festival Week. Their idea – for a full day of music and arts on the final day, called after the old name for St Just – has grown like topsy.

Every venue in St Just is in action. The centre of the town is closed to traffic. Local traders and stallholders set up a wonderful variety of stands. Streets fill with spectacular, noisy, happy processions. Giant images, flags and banners are produced by school and youth groups, in creative workshops led by local artists. Bands and groups sing and play in Market Square and the Plen-an-Gwary, and street performers entertain throughout the day.

Colour and light, music and laughter and, with any luck, sunshine!

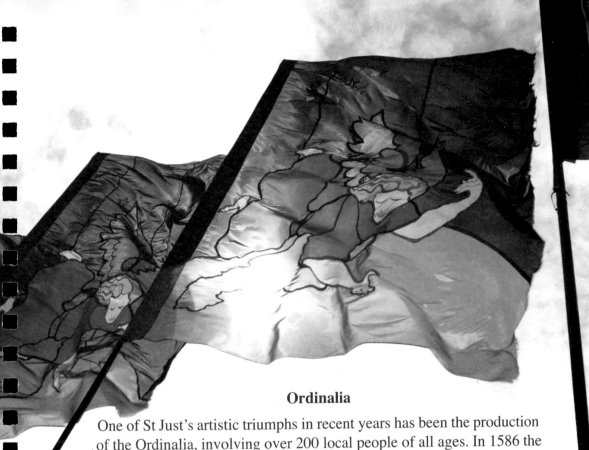

Ordinalia

One of St Just's artistic triumphs in recent years has been the production of the Ordinalia, involving over 200 local people of all ages. In 1586 the High Sheriff of Cornwall, having seen a production, announced that *'it had devices to delight as well the eye as the ear'* – and indeed it still has.

Written in Cornish in the late 14th century by the monks of Glasney College, Penryn, as a means of teaching Bible stories to ordinary people, the Ordinalia is in three parts and was designed for staging outdoors. The Plen-an-Gwary, possibly the oldest continually used performing area in the country, would almost certainly have seen early productions of the Ordinalia.

It was there in 2000 that the Ordinalia Company gave its first performance. *Origo Mundi,* the story of the Creation, was followed in subsequent years by the *Passion* and the *Resurrection*. In 2004 the Trilogy was performed as a single, complete play. Translated into modern English by Pauline Sheppard, with original music and stunning sets, the result was a spectacular success bringing visitors from all over the country.

Cape Sports

With fine, settled weather and no great swell running in, you have the perfect ingredients for the annual Cape Sports. The main feature is the arduous Brisons Swim. Local fishermen take competitors out to the starting point, a mile offshore for adults. So fit are the swimmers that the winners finish in less than 20 minutes. There are two other races – a half and a quarter swim for younger racers. A thick layer of grease, stamina and determination bring you ashore. Families and visitors gather on the beach. Barbeques sizzle, boat trips round the Brisons are organized, and, after the Swim, Vikings invade, to be greeted with a barrage of flour bombs.

Cape Sports follows an ancient tradition, as this account shows:

At two o'clock the same day we passed between the Wolf and the Longships, then on, passing the Brissons about two miles out.
It was Midsummer day, and I thought probably the St. Just folk are having Regatta; I plainly saw 4 or 5 boats very close together, under sail. I think I might have prevailed on our Capt. to have allowed us to land at Priest Cove, but knowing he wanted to save the tide in at Liverpool, and had on board mails that ought not to be delayed, I did not ask him to grant the boon.
We contented ourselves with looking at the people, and the old home through our glasses, as we steamed northward to Liverpool, we landed the following day, after a pleasant voyage of 42 days from Valparaiso.

Conclusion of Grandfather Trahair's talk about his life in South America 1847-1885, given to the St Just Institution
4th March 1887

In the lee of a rock above Progo, sheltering from a rain-squall

Wind: West-South-West Force 8

Visibility: Good. Poor in squally showers

Barometer: 996 falling

Racing in from the Scillies
a cotton-wool cloud rolls up the ocean
in a ragged grey curtain,
driven by the cold, hard, polar air stream.

Jackdaws, blown inside out
like bundles of black rags,
dive over the cliff edge
in jumbles of feathers, beaks and legs.

The line-squall whips inshore,
seeking out zawns and valleys,
blinding the Longships and cliffs to the South,
lifting above the sheltering rock
to sweep up Cot.

When it clears, the sky is washed and clean.
Cliffs glisten wetly.
The voluptuous curves
of Little Sandy's beaten rocks beckon.

If it's cold, wet and windy outside.
Then the Cook Book is where you must hide.
Taste our soup steaming hot
In a Helen Joy pot.
And stay till you've warmed up and dried.

Soup

Soup is one of The Cook Book's most popular lines. As regular customers will know, our soups vary with the seasons, the availability of vegetables and the mood of the cook. We love experimenting with combinations of different seasonal vegetables, spices and herbs.

Most soups are suitable for vegetarians.

Amongst our regular soup-eaters we have a growing number of discerning pupils from Cape Cornwall School.

"The ability to make soup is the test of a good cook"

Winston Churchill
December 1940

Red Root Soup

Start with an onion, chopped and sautéed gently until soft
Chop equal quantities of beetroot, carrot, parsnip and potato
Sweet potato and swede can also be included
Add the vegetables to the onion
Sprinkle with some dried thyme
Mix well and add vegetable stock to cover the vegetables
Bring to the boil and then simmer until the vegetables are cooked
Liquidize, season with salt and pepper. A dollop of ketchup is a nice addition

Courgette and Cheese Soup

1 onion
2 medium potatoes
650g (1½lb) courgettes
850mls (1½ pints) vegetable stock
125g (4oz) cheese – Stilton or Cheddar – grated

Sauté the chopped onion and potatoes for a few minutes
Add the stock
Bring to the boil and simmer gently
When the potatoes are nearly cooked, add the courgettes and continue cooking
until they are soft
Leave the lid off. This will help retain the colour of the courgettes
Liquidize and stir in the cheese
Season to taste

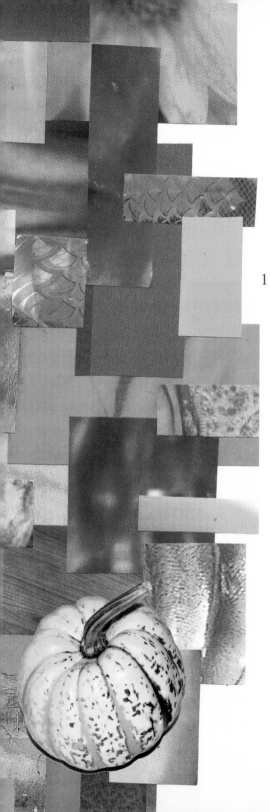

Pumpkin or Squash, Carrot and Ginger

1½ kilo (3lb) pumpkin, peeled & pipped
1 kilo (2lb) carrot, topped, tailed & scrubbed
3 large onions
1 tbsp of grated ginger root

Chop vegetables
Sauté onions until soft
Add ginger
Add vegetables
Cook on a medium heat
Add vegetable stock and
2-3 litres (4-5 pints) hot water
Cook till soft
Whizzle

This makes a lot of soup!

Broccoli and Almond Soup

1 onion, sautéed until soft
1 head of fresh broccoli
3 medium potatoes
Ground almonds

Chop potato and add to the onion
When beginning to cook, add the broccoli broken into florets
Cover with vegetable stock
Cook gently until the potatoes are soft
Stir in two tablespoons of ground almonds (or to taste)
Blend, season and serve with roasted flaked almonds

*I feel I must wax sentimental
On the simple and nourishing lentil.
In the soup with tomato
It far beats potato:
An experience quite existential*

Lentil and Tomato Soup

1 onion
250g (8oz) lentils
1 tin chopped tomatoes
1 tbsp tomato ketchup
1 litre (1½ pints) of vegetable stock

Chop onion and cook gently until soft
Add the lentils, tomatoes, stock and ketchup
Bring to the boil and simmer till lentils are soft
Liquidize and season

Pea, Bean and Bacon Soup

1 onion
1 stick of celery
1 leek
3 rashers of streaky bacon
2 bags of frozen peas
1 bag of frozen broad beans
Bay leaf
Pinch of thyme (fresh or dried)
Vegetable stock

Chop up onions, celery, leek and bacon

Fry bacon till the fat runs
Add celery, leek and onion to the bacon
Cook for a few minutes
Add 1000ml (2 pints) of vegetable stock and the herbs
When vegetables are nearly soft, add peas and beans
Simmer for 15 minutes
Do not over cook
Liquidise to a thick porridge
Check seasoning and serve

In March 1869 The Board of Trade made a provisional order to the St Just Harbour & Pier Co. to build a harbour and basin at Penanwell (Porth Nanven) at a cost of £48,000.

Quiche On The Wind

With a tiny galley in the fo'c'stle of our first home, a 60ft old gaffer, the cook had a bumpy ride. We only had a small fixed cooker, without the luxury of gimbals. All hot water had to be boiled, so the kettle would be lashed down to stop it flying about, as were any pans on the top burners. Wire coat hangers were excellent for this.

Cooking for fourteen souls at sea under sail was an exercise in organisation, balance and dogged determination.

We always had a cooked breakfast; soup and sandwiches or quiche for lunch, and a big evening meal – meat and three vegetables and a pudding, plus endless cups of tea at all hours.

The Cook Book kitchen is small but palatial compared to cooking afloat – and quiches don't end up sloping at odd angles.

Ken Symonds

Our favourite – Bacon, Brie and Cranberry Sauce Baguette

Warm a baguette
Split along the top – not right through – and butter
Put generous slices of Cornish Brie in the baguette
Grill or fry two or three rashers of bacon
While bacon is cooking, lightly grill the Brie
Remove baguette and Brie from the grill
Put a layer of cranberry sauce on top of the melted Brie
Put the bacon on top of that and serve with an elegant side salad

Cornish Brie

This is a wonderfully soft and creamy full fat cheese churned at The Creamery, Trevarrian and supplied to us by Rodda's. It is best served at room temperature and eaten in large quantities

Try a Nova Scotia

Take a thick slice of bread
Cut a round hole in the middle about 1½ inches in diameter
Place the bread and the cut out piece in hot fat (bacon is best) or in hot oil
Break an egg into the hole
Fry on one side
Turn over and cook on the other side. *Serve with bacon, beans and tomatoes*

A great snack is Cheesy Garlic Beans on Toast

Heat a small tin of baked beans with a clove of crushed garlic
Spread on hot buttered toast
Thickly cover with grated cheese
Sprinkle with a little Worcestershire sauce and grill

Homity Pie

Pastry ingredients

175g (6oz) plain flour
50g (2oz) grated Parmesan cheese
125g (4oz) unsalted butter
1 medium egg
1 tbsp of olive oil

Crumble the butter in the flour and Parmesan cheese
Make a well in the centre
Break in the egg and add oil
Mix with a knife
Refrigerate for at least one hour before using
Roll out the pastry
Put in an 8 inch greased flan dish
Bake blind for about 15 minutes in a hot oven

Filling ingredients

350g (¾lb) potatoes cooked and mashed
500g (1 lb) onions cooked slowly in oil until soft and glazed
25g (1oz) butter
15g (½oz) chopped parsley
100g (4oz) grated cheese
2 cloves of garlic crushed
1 tbsp milk
Seasoning

Mix all the ingredients together and season – the amount of cheese and garlic
may be adjusted to your palate. Place filling into pastry case and bake in a
moderate oven for approximately 20 minutes

Alsia Cross Salad Leaves

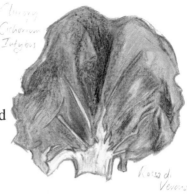

Mizuna

Salad Rocket

Giant Red Mustard

Tatsoi

Pak Choi

Endive

Chicory

Three Cornered Leek

Corn Salad

Nasturtium Flowers

Borage Flowers

Parsley

Red Cabbage

Miners' Lettuce

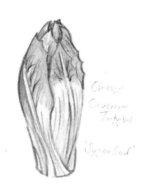

There is much competition to produce the prettiest salad

Jo's Vinaigrette

3 parts extra virgin olive oil – approximately 300ml (½ pint)
1 part white wine vinegar – approximately 100ml
Juice of one lemon
1 heaped dessertspoon of mustard
1 heaped tablespoon of cranberry sauce
4 cloves of peeled garlic
1 level dessertspoon of Demerara sugar

Crush garlic and put in a glass jar with a good lid
Add olive oil and shake
Add white wine vinegar to taste. Shake
Add lemon juice to taste. Shake
Add mustard, cranberry sauce and sugar, tasting as you go
Shake well before serving

Looking across Cot Valley in July

Wind: Calm

Visibility: 300 feet

Barometer: 1013 steady

A slow moving warm front
settles clammy, wet wool
blanketing Cot Valley in a thick St Juster.
Mist clings persistently to cliffs,
blurring edges,
filling zawns, adits, shafts,
stifling the stream,
muffling the Longships warning whistle.

Aircraft and birds are grounded.

Fingers of fog feel through houses,
mildewing leather,
dampening clothes, paper, bedding,
settling rust on ironwork and
verdigris on dulled brass fenders.

Dew glints in diffused grey light
Etching spiders' silken webs
in shivering silver crystal,
Softening gorse needles, bowing bracken,
dripping from lichen-clothed trees and still leaves.

Another summer day.

The restless sea washes across empty beaches.

Bren Unwin

Cream Teas

Cream teas are a West Country phenomenon, but they are constantly being hijacked up-country. I met one in Edinburgh a year or so ago. Being in Scotland the scones were delicious, the jam passable: but the cream – oh dear – a nasty squirt of something that looked and tasted like shaving foam.

Here at The Cook book our cream teas are truly West Country – vital ingredient clotted cream – and truly Cornish – vital ingredient Saffron Bun.

The strawberry jam is packed with fruit and is especially delicious. It is traditionally made every summer on the Boddington's family farm at Mevagissey, using only hand picked, fresh strawberries that are cooked within 48 hours of picking. Only lemon juice and sugar is added. You can buy Boddington's jam here and take a taste of Cornwall home with you.

Our scones are home-made. There is a good choice of different teas. Saffron buns come from Warren's Bakery here in St Just, and Rodda's of Scorrier supply us with our clotted cream.

I hope that by now you'll have spotted
That the cream on your scone must be clotted.
Is it jam first, cream next?
'Tis a question most vexed.
Tick the box in the small square allotted!

Cream ☐   Jam ☐

We conducted a straw poll amongst our customers and came to no conclusion at all!

Saffron Buns

Saffron, a member of the of the iris family (crocus satirus), has been used commercially since classical times. We are familiar with it as a dye in the orange robes of Buddhist monks; the ancient Egyptians incorporated it in cosmetic ranges; and as a spice it is familiar in Spanish paella and in many Indian dishes.

The crocus, from which the three-pronged style or "saffron" is plucked, flowers in the autumn and has to be harvested by hand. Hence its high price. I have seen fields of these delicate mauve flowers – brilliant orange threads in each one, ready for plucking – in Kashmir, in the foothills of the Himalayas.

Saffron probably arrived in Cornwall with the tin-trading Phoenicians. It has become a part of the Cornish diet in the form of fruity dough buns and cakes incorporating strands of saffron for flavour and colour.

The saffron bun that we serve as part of your cream tea can be eaten on its own or with cream. It can also be toasted, and it makes a delicious snack with butter and cheddar cheese.

Saffron
Crocus Sativus

Children and Dogs

The Cook Book is really child friendly. We have high chairs, toys – the favourite is a musical dog featuring "Singing in the Rain." We can heat up bottles in the microwave or make special small meals and sandwiches. For the newborn, one of our large bread baskets makes an excellent cradle.

The children's section of the Book Shop is popular and the thunder of tiny feet upstairs in the book rooms is a regular feature of family visits. Best of all is the total silence when a child has found a book and is lying on the floor, wholly engrossed.

We are also animal friendly. At present all our animal regulars are dogs, though we did have a horse visiting on one occasion, but only outside while its owner had an ice-cream. We are broadminded and would be happy to welcome any animals provided they are not of a size to be lost in the store cupboard.

All visiting dogs get a small piece of cheese and thereafter drag their owners into the café whenever they are in the area. This is good for trade…

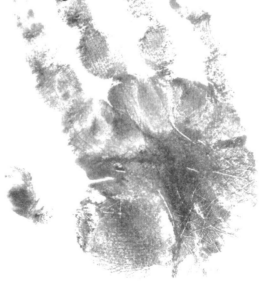

Luke – aged 17 months

The Book Rest
Book Bites ?
The Feed and Read
Bibliomania Café
Bibliocafé
* Bistro Bookshop
The Cook Book
Book Browsers Café
Tasty Tomes
Literary Lunch
The Book
Café and Books
The Bookworm Eats
Café au Livre
Chew over a Book

A late afternoon November walk around the valley

Wind: East-South-East Force 2

Sea State: Slight

Visibility: Good

Barometer: 1015 falling slowly

On this still November day
silence balloons across the zawn,
broken only by the mine stream's
restless chuckling chatter
as it rushes to meet the sea.

Bones of the worked-out hillside
push against wind-stripped
rust-red bracken and flayed,
ruby stems of salt-bleached brambles.

Dark, green, lustrous ivy squeezes
crumbling walls, sheltering
a worked quillet,
rare sign of industry.
Fresh minted gold of winter gorse
gleams among tumbled burrows
of shattered granite.

Only the mine stream is busily constant,
filling the still air with music
echoing across
the hollowed-out, wind-scoured valley.

Carrie Taylor

Turn Left at the Clock Tower

…but it is a memorial to the 78 sons of this town killed in two world wars.

Designed by Henry Thomas, Chairman of the St Just War Memorial Committee, and built by John Angwin and William Trezise. It was unveiled in August 1931 by The Hon. W.C. Angwin, Agent General for Western Australia.

The clock came from Smith's of London.

Surprisingly, it was not built in granite. That was too expensive during the post war depression.

4 Cape Cornwall Street was built in the late 18th Century. In living memory it has been a private home, Perrow's sweet shop, a ladies hairdresser and St Just Tea Rooms. When Number 4 was built, there was a coffee shop and booksellers in Cape Cornwall Street. We don't know where, but it feels good to have an historic precedent. The old building behind used to be Angwin's slaughter house.

Alfie Olds, who lives almost opposite, was the local milkman until 1997. His cows grazed in Home Fields until 1964/5. These are now the car park and Lafrowda Close. Alfie milked in the parlour, still standing at the end of West Place. His dairy was behind 24 Cape Cornwall Street, the family home since 1840. Boswedden Road used to be called Angle Street – at one time it had two slaughter houses, a dairy, and a stable and harness house. This became a fire station and is now a private house. One slaughter house is still working there.

The big building on the seaward side is the Bolitho Working Men's Club. In its time it has housed a library and the town cinema. It had a magnificent wooden balcony.

In 1885 Philippa's great-grandfather Trahair began a series of talks there about working and travelling in South America. The first was called:

A description of three year's rambles in the Republic of Chile.

On the 2nd day of April 1849, I left St. Just, to find my way to far off South America; I was almost the first to leave for a foreign land, so a great many came to see me off, to say "good bye", for they thought I should never come back again.
On the top of Treguney, I turned, like the soldier, to take a last fond look of the old place, with a tear in my eye, I shall never forget it, for I was leaving all that was near and dear to me, to seek a strange land, where no familiar face would meet my eye, where a strange language should fall on my ear, not understood............

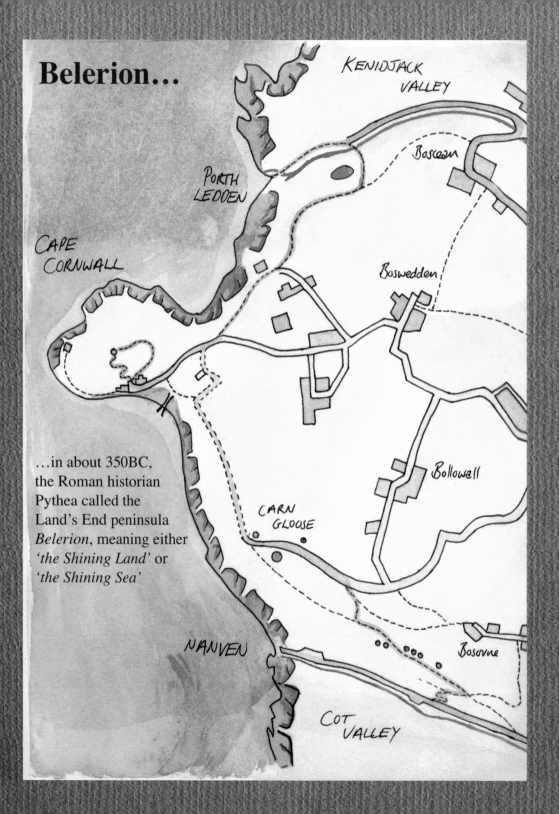

Belerion...

...in about 350BC, the Roman historian Pythea called the Land's End peninsula *Belerion*, meaning either *'the Shining Land'* or *'the Shining Sea'*

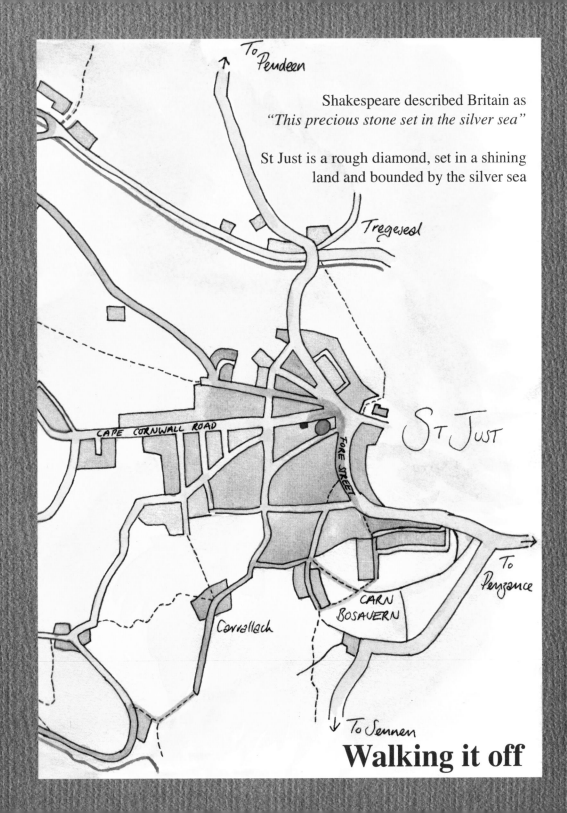

To Pendeen

Shakespeare described Britain as
"This precious stone set in the silver sea"

St Just is a rough diamond, set in a shining
land and bounded by the silver sea

Tregeseal

CAPE CORNWALL ROAD

FORE STREET

St Just

To Penzance

Carvallack

CARN BOSAVERN

To Sennen

Walking it off

Walk 1   Café – Carn Bosavern

Time: 10 – 15 minutes, depending on how long your legs are

An easy walk for all, although it can be slippery and muddy if wet

Turn right towards the centre of St Just. Go past the War Memorial, the Co-op and the Commercial Hotel until you reach Fore Street. Walk up the street on the right-hand-side – tread carefully as the pavement is very narrow. Keep on going, past St Just Garage, across the entrance to South Place to where the main road turns left up the hill – at the corner, on the right-hand, there is a small set of steps leading to a narrow lane.

Go up the steps, along the lane, to the T-junction. Turn left and then immediately right, between No. 33 and No. 34, into another short lane. This will bring you onto the road leading up to Carn Bosavern. Walk to the top of this road and take a right across a stony car park. Follow the path and climb over a low wall – there are makeshift steps, but take care.

Once over the wall, take either the left or the right route until you reach the rocks themselves.

Facing seaward, to your right lies the town of St Just from on high, to your left, the vast countryside.

Extra care must be taken with children, as the rocks can be slippery when wet. It is open to high winds!

You can return via the route you came by.

*If you want to extend your walk via the coast paths, follow **Walks 2, 3, 4 and 5.** These take you on a circular route of great interest and beauty. Each walk can also start and finish at The Cook Book, where, naturally, we are always delighted to welcome you.*

St Just Church

War Memorial

Bank Square

Cape Cornwell Road

THE COOK BOOK – PLEN-AN-GWARY

Market Square

Public Toilets

Bus Stop

Free Parking

FORE STREET

SOUTH PLACE

To Penzance

N°34 N°33

To Carralleck

CARN BOSAVERN

Walk 2   Carn Bosavern – Cot Valley

Time: 45 minutes, approximately

An easy route but take care on the narrow roads. Some muddy terrain

There are two footpaths on the seaward side of the Carn, one going straight down and the other over a low wall to the North. Both take you to a road. Take care, as the paths can be slippery if muddy. At the bottom of either path, take a right leading onto the road, followed by a left, into Carrallack Lane. Follow this downhill until you reach a junction at the bottom. The main road curves to the right. You take a left, following the tarmac farm road all the way to the end, where there is a bench if you need it! There is a breathtaking view of the **Brisons**.

To the right is **"Scrabbly" Lane**. Follow this to the bottom, but take care, this is fairly uneven and a moderate descent. At the bottom, take a right along a muddy footpath leading to a road. Note the beautiful garden on your left. Take a left downhill but beware of traffic (very little) and the steep, blind corner.

You are now in **Cot Valley**. Follow the road to the sea, taking in the scenery – plants, stream, wildlife and particularly the old mine workings. Do not tread off the stated paths as unmarked shafts lurk in the undergrowth. The road ends at a small sand and boulder beach, **Penanwell**, also known as Nanven, with its distinctive **Putty Rock** and rounded stones. For the adventurous, a coastal path leads to **Sennen** to the South. Take care as the sea can be extremely dangerous on a rough day and the coast path becomes slippery.

There is a legend that Joseph of Arimathaea and the boy Jesus landed at Penanwell and walked up Cot Valley on their way to Glastonbury.

To return to St Just, either follow the road all the way, approximately 30 minutes, or follow the next route, **Walk 3** to **Carn Gloose**, with magnificent views of the surrounding coast.

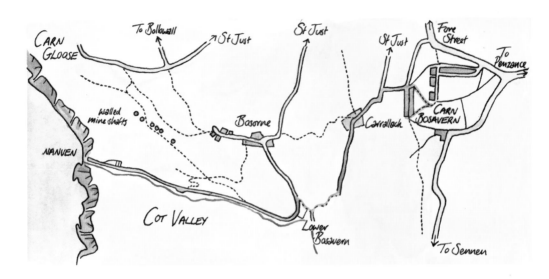

Gentle Walk from The Cook Book to Cot Valley – *approximately 30 minutes*

Turn left towards the sea. Turn left at **The Old Sunday School**, following the sign for Cot Valley – **The Great Atlantic Gallery** is on your right, then **St Just Primary School**. Follow Bosorne Road down hill, out of town to **Cot Valley**. The way is sign posted and the going easy. Beware of traffic.

Walk 3   Cot Valley – Carn Gloose

Time: 20 – 30 minutes, approximately

This is a fairly stiff walk for children and the elderly with steep and uneven paths, but the breathtaking views more than make up for the journey

Head back up the road from **Penanwell** for approximately 4 – 500 yards, until you reach a public footpath to your left, leading up the North side of the valley. Go up some rocky steps, then head inland along a grass track until you reach the foot of the steep, stony and uneven path going uphill to the left. Follow this to the top, stopping at obvious intervals to take in the view.

On the way you will notice old mine shafts surrounded by stone walls. Don't stray too far off the path. There are numerous hidden shafts in the undergrowth.

Over many years **Willy Olds** built the granite benches along this and other paths around Cot Valley and to the South.

When you reach the top of the path, take either a left or a right. The left route carries on along the coast path, bringing you to the end of the cliff with a magnificent view… and a bench to sit on if you are shattered!

The right route leads straight on to the road, which is relatively flat. Take a left and follow the road to the end. Just past the chimney stack you will see the ancient **Bollowall Barrow** on your left, well worth climbing onto and exploring.

There is an Ordnance Survey trig point, now redundant, on the right. Almost opposite are some low walls and a flat area with a picnic table in it. These are the remains of the nineteenth century gun emplacement of the **Cape Cornwall Volunteer Artillery Battery** that protected the beaches from invasion.

To get back to St Just from here if you have had enough, follow the road all the way back until you reach the **Bryan Warren Cricket Pavilion.** Note the weather vane, designed and built by our son Jake! Turn right at the Pavilion and follow the road all the way back to the top. Note The Cook Book on your right if you fancy a nice cream tea! **In reverse, this is the gentle walk to Carn Gloose**.

White
Gate

CARN GLOOSE

To
Bollowall

To
St Just

Bollowall
Barrow

Chimney
Stack

NANVEN

Walled
Mine
Shafts

Basorne

Old Mine
Workings

COT
VALLEY

If you are willing to carry
on, follow **Walk 4** to **Cape
Cornwall** and **Priest's Cove**

Walk 4   Carn Gloose – Cape Cornwall

Time: 20 – 25 minutes, approximately

A moderate and stony descent, suitable for most with care

Standing on Carn Gloose facing Cape Cornwall, there is a granite stile on the left of an old gateway – still known as **The White Gate**. The track leads down hill towards Cape Cornwall. Follow it to the bottom. On the way you pass two cottages, site of the famous **St Just United Mines**.

At the bottom you can either follow the track up hill to the road, leading to **Cape Cornwall**, or turn sharp left towards **Priest's Cove**. If you go up the track, turn left at the road. There are **public toilets** (not open all year) in the National Trust car park on your left. Go down the road and onto the Cape, the most Westerly point of England. On top, accessible by two footpaths, is an old mine stack. From there you will have fantastic views, well worth the climb. To seaward is the **National Coastwatch Lookout**, easily accessible from the South side of the Cape by path and steps, except in a gale of wind, when great care must be taken.

To the South is **Priest's Cove**, with a slipway, fishermen's huts, cove boats, winch house, and small stony beach with a natural swimming pool built into the rocks. The slipway and rocks can be very slippery, especially when the tide is going out. Fishermen work from here when weather and sea state permit.

Returning to St Just on the road is not recommended for it is narrow, the corners are blind and, during peak season, traffic is heavy.

Instead, go uphill on the road, past **Porthledden House** to your left and the **Golf Club** on your right, until you come to **Boswedden Hotel** on your left. Turn left in here onto a stony road. Turn right past the hotel, over a stile and into fields with a footpath running along the right hand side. Follow this through all three fields, over stiles, until you reach a gate and stile. Climb the stile onto a farm track and, eventually, a tarmac road. Continue uphill into St Just where you will emerge by the War Memorial. **In reverse, this is an easy route to Cape Cornwall**, taking about 25 minutes downhill – and longer coming up the gentle slopes.

If you still feel fit, follow Walk 5 for an interesting walk into another valley.

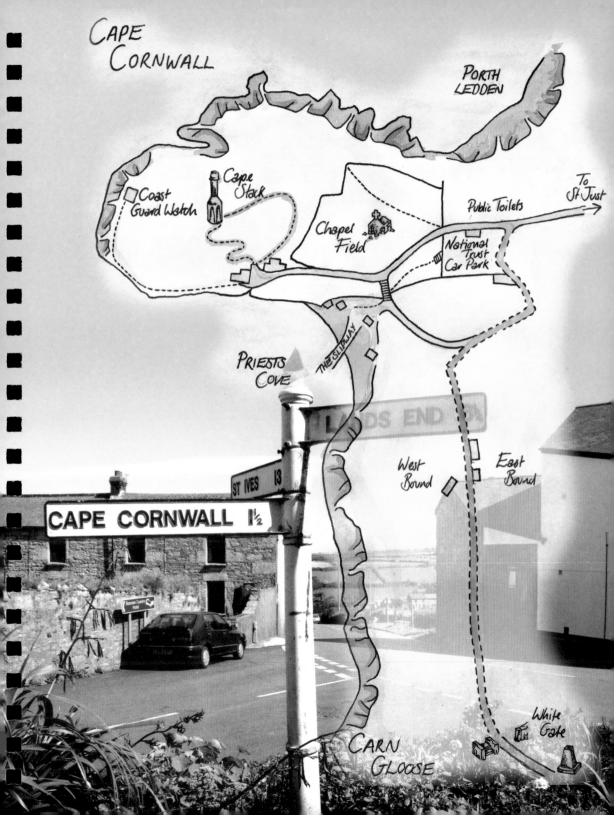

Walk 5   Cape Cornwall – Kenidjack Valley

Time: 45 – 60 minutes, approximately

Moderate to steep descent on well-defined track. Can be muddy

Go up the hill on the road until opposite the National Trust car park. Take a left along a track running in front of **Porthledden House**, a magnificent building on your right, built in about 1907 by a mining friend of Cecil Rhodes, **Captain Oates**, in the style of Rhodes' house in South Africa, Groet Schoer. Go on past a white house built on the edge of the cliff, until the track forks. Take the left-hand path and keep going along it until a steep track descends to your left. Take this to go down into the valley, or follow on straight ahead until you reach a farmyard and the road back into St Just.

Descending into the valley, to your left is a rebuilt pond and to the right, rebuilt mine buildings. Keeping on the path, go over a stream on a wooden footbridge. The small fields to your left often have friendly donkeys in them. Then you have a choice. Take a left and follow the stream to its mouth in **Porth Ledden**. (You will notice a footpath leading up the hill on the North slope. This leads to the **Crown Mines, Zennor** and beyond…well worth walking.)

The path to the sea is good going amongst dramatic scenery, with many remains of old mine workings. You have to jump across the stream near the sea. Take care with children, as the rocks are slippery. At low tide, and with care, unless you are a good rock-hopper, you can make your way across the cove to Cape Cornwall. You will often see seals here.

Take a right and the track gradually ascends until you come to cottages on your left and a bridge to your right. Cross the bridge and follow the track up hill. It joins a road by **Boscean Pottery** and a farmyard. Follow this road back into St Just, coming out opposite the War Memorial.

Take this walk in reverse from The Cook Book.

KENIDJACK VALLEY

PORTH LEDDEN

pond

To Botallack

Boscean

Pottery

To Cape
Cornwall

Porthledden
House

Boswedden

Tregeseal

National
Trust
Car Park

ST JUST

to Carn
Gloose

Bollowall

To Basorne
and Cot Valley

Dog Fox At Bosorne

Crouching low,
moulded to the
turf-topped hedge,
his bracken-red winter coat,
freshly washed by
days of driving rain,
fluffed out, drying
in the windless evening sun.

Staring intently
with wide-set eyes wide open
fixed on mine,
ears pricked forward,
one front paw
tucked to his shoulder,
the other stretched down,
pressed against the stone.

Flowing up the wall
in a silent blur,
he paused in the quillet,
glanced back;
and was gone –
with awkward stumbling gait
alien to his natural fluid grace,
an injured paw
slowing his homeward run.

The dogs whimpered, straining to hunt him down.

Bosorne Books

On a search for your favourite book?
Then the Cook Book is where you must look.
We have books on the stairs,
The tables and chairs
And in every available nook

About Bosorne Books

We have about 4,500 second-hand books, sorted by genre, in two rooms upstairs, and an eclectic selection downstairs.

Books everywhere!

Buying them is easy. Parting with books before we have read them is difficult. We love books.

Browsers will note that we have very little modern hard-back fiction – just those that may become classics. However, we do have a good selection of paper-back fiction. Ideal holiday reading.

As we learn more about buying and selling books, so we aim to improve the quality of our stock for the general reader. We were real greenhorns when we started. Having wonderful friends at the Helston Bookworm, Ann and Malcolm Summers, we were able to learn the book trade at their knees without making too many mistakes. David spent a week running their shop while they were on holiday; days were spent assessing book values with them, as well as learning basic book care and repair.

It was Ann and Malcolm, and their friends John and Pearl Lewis, who stocked Bosorne Books from scratch. They bought 4,500 books for us and we did not know what they were. Unpacking the boxes was like a glorious Christmas treat!

I hope that the books are selling like hot cakes,
and the hot cakes are being digested like good books
– and it's still fun.

Jeremy Alexander
The Guardian

Bosorne Books is so-called because we live in Bosorne!

Apart from second-hand books, we also sell Evocative Cornwall Calendars and Christmas cards, jb hand-made soaps and a small selection of cards.

Bren Unwin

Cooks and Books

Philippa James

Cornish. Worked on a farm, learned cooking, clerked about, travelled to Africa, India and the Far East. Worked in Hong Kong in 1969 where she met David. In London in 1975, he re-appeared, in sea boots and a sou'wester! Married soon after a freezing voyage down Channel. Lived onboard *Larvik* in the West India Docks, taking young East Enders to sea. Cook, deck hand, watch-keeper and wife. Two children, Jake and Ellie; every holiday at the family home in Bosorne; multiple sclerosis; back to Cornwall. Penwith College for 'A' Level Religious Studies. …"would I be foolish to think of going to university?" Edinburgh, four fantastic years, including a summer semester at Dartmouth College, New Hampshire; 2:1 MA. Caring for an aged mother … and now The Cook Book.

David James

A sailor from a service family. Royal Navy for eight happy years, then four lean years working up from boat yard skivvy to skipper, via fish packing, yacht deliveries and running a sailing school. Skippered a gaff ketch for 2½ years. Came ashore. Ran Ocean Youth Club for nine seasons, then two other national youth charities before working for people with disabilities in Cornwall. Redundancy led to Cape Cornwall School…
and from there to The Cook Book.

Caroline Binch

Jenny Stephens

A true St Just lady, mother and grandmother, Jenny taught herself to cook and has always enjoyed baking. She makes nearly all the cakes we sell. Her husband, Paul, is a member of the Longships and Cape Singers and Jenny travels with them. She "enjoys running The Cook Book when David and Philippa are away".

The Cook Book Crew

One of the most attractive features of The Cook Book is the small army of the brightest and best of St Just and Pendeen who work for us.

When we opened, we were at the bottom of a steep learning curve. We were carried and cajoled by Rosie P and Gemma, whom we inherited from the former owners. Without them we would have been floundering. These two, together with Ben and Rosie S, were the experienced quorum who knew how the café worked.

Thereafter, scarcely a week went by but someone dropped in on the way to or from school, to ask if there was any work available. Thus we acquired Jo, Morwenna, Rosenwyn, Rachel, Danielle and Clare. Jenny's daughter, Natalie joined the team with her youngest son Kieran, who generally supervises all that goes on from his high chair. Then Lottie, Jess and Matthew found their way to our door. Our most recent school recruit is Charlie, who followed our two artists, Stella and Daisy.

An army indeed! There are far too many of them. They eat their way – often literally through mountains of chocolate fudge cake – into our profits. We love them dearly and so do our customers.

Book People

Born in Cornwall, **Stella Billingham-Henderson** is our in-house designer. She is creative, musical, artistic – and the finest cappuccino frother in West Penwith. **Daisy Gibbs** is our illustrator. She's proper Cornish, knows just about everyone locally and has a particular interest in stage and set design.

The editors are delighted and grateful to have the enthusiastic support of the following contributors, who retain copyright of their individual work:

Artists:
Ken Symonds has lived and worked in Cornwall for many years: widely travelled and as comfortable with landscapes as with nudes, portraits or still life. **Neil Pinkett** grew up in St Just: a leading contemporary landscape artist with a penchant for the moors and cliffs of the Land's End Peninsula and any aspect of the Isles of Scilly. **Bren Unwin** first came to St Just in the 1960's: a member of The Royal Society of Painter-Printmakers, her work makes an enquiry into how time operates in the landscape. **Carrie Taylor** lives in St Just: she paints intuitively, responding to the richness and rough-edged beauty of the Penwith landscape, blending her observations with a lifelong fascination with natural history. **Caroline Binch** is a children's book illustrator, writer and photographer. She lives near the sea with four dogs, a cat and a feller.
Photography: mostly by **Don Kirk**, habitué of The Cook Book. He has a wonderful eye for the unusual. **Tom Henderson Smith.**
Walks: Ben Rowell, super-fit student at Penwith College and joining the Royal Marines. Works at The Cook Book.
Maps: Stella Billingham-Henderson and **Daisy Gibbs**
Poetry: David James and **John Gordon**.

Written by **Philippa and David James**, who remain married even after some extremely rude comments about each other's literary style and taste! (If you would like samples of Philippa's tasteless prose, please send her a plain brown stamped addressed envelope. David's is best left unprinted.)

Edited by Philippa, David, Stella and Daisy, without any arguments at all.